MW00451574

Courage to Persevere

A Compelling Story of Struggle, Survival, and Triumph

Tami
Gilbert

Dream World Press Publishing

Copyright ©2015 Tami Gilbert

Published in the United States of America
by
Dream World Press Publishing

ISBN: 978-0-9967765-0-9

Cover Picture: Anre J. Brownlee

Professional Wedding Pictures: Steve Neilson

All rights reserved. No part of this book may be used or reproduced by any means, graphic,
electronic, or mechanical, including photocopying, recording, taping or by any information
storage retrieval system without the written permission of the publisher or author except in
the case of brief quotations embodied in critical articles and reviews.

Table of Contents

Why I Wrote this Book

One Woman's Journey

I was born in Nigeria, the western part of the continent of Africa. When I was seven or eight years old—a tiny little girl, barefoot and displaced—my father left to go to Chicago. Then, a few years later, my mother left as well to go back to her hometown in a different part of Africa. Abandoned by both my father and mother, I was left to be raised by my elderly aunt and grandmother. When I was fifteen years of age, my father sent for me, my sister, and brother to come to Chicago. I was so excited! I left Nigeria and flew to this new, big city in a strange country to finally live with my father.

Once I arrived, my dream was shattered when my father sent me and my sister to live with my young cousin instead. My cousin had also emigrated from Nigeria a few years earlier, and I barely knew him. When we arrived at his house, it was clear we were not wanted there. I was already very upset about being abandoned for a second time by my father; I had been hopeful that here, perhaps, could be a new family for me. But instead of being given a cozy, upstairs bedroom, we had to live in the cold, dimly lit, concrete basement. Those were dark days.

One night, as I lay in my tiny bed with my sister, shivering and cold, unable to fall asleep, I made this decree: "I will do whatever it takes to get out of here." I knew that the key was getting an education so I could afford a warm place to live. That was the moment where I decided to pursue a college degree. I did get into college but found it difficult to stay there because I didn't have enough money to pay for tuition. But I was determined not to let anything stand in my way.

In fact, I refused to let any obstacles stop me from achieving my goals. I worked two jobs as a nurse's assistant to pay for my tuition, and eventually I got my bachelor of science in nursing. But I had bigger dreams than that. I wanted the best life possible so that I would never have to be cold and hungry again. So, I went back to school to get my

1

Masters of Science in Nursing and Masters of Business Administration, and after a lot of hard work, I got those degrees as well. I am also an authorized Occupational Safety and Health (OSHA) Trainer and ServSafe Food Sanitation Safety Trainer.

After my struggles to get my education, I thought I had finally arrived in my dream land. I got a job with one of the biggest teaching hospitals in Chicago; that was when I discovered racism in corporate America. I could not move up the ladder; I was only able to get positions that did not require an advanced degree. Not able to work up to my potential and belittled, I decided I was going to do everything in my power to find another job. Thanks to a friend who helped me get an interview, plus a lot of research and preparation on my part, I soon got a much better job as a surgical clinical coordinator.

By this time, after getting my nursing degree, I had saved enough money to own a cozy condo in downtown Chicago and had gotten out of that dark, cold, concrete basement forever. But then I found myself without anybody to share my life with. Every night, I came back from work to an empty house when what I really wanted was a home. I had spent so many years getting my education and finding work that once I accomplished those goals, I realized I was lonely and wanted to have a family. These feelings were all the more intense during the holidays when I watched family movies on television. I would go out hoping to meet that special someone, and I even was open to going out on blind dates.

One day, I was set up on a blind date, and we met at a small cafe, sat at a table next to a window, ordered sandwiches, and talked and talked and talked. I looked across the table at him: average build, red hair, not too tall, nice looking, and I was captivated by his warm smile and deep voice. Scott had two kids from a previous marriage, and the way he spoke about them made me realize that he was family oriented, and right then I knew I was going to marry him. A year after we met, he proposed, and we married a year later. Together, we now have three children.

It's been quite a journey. I have a fulfilling career, am happily married with a family, and now I am here to help others overcome their obstacles and achieve their dreams. I am here to tell you that with perseverance, you can be successful at anything that you put your mind to. You are not alone. You can be in charge of your life, and you do not have to live a life of disappointment.

So this is my story, and for a long time, I thought about writing a book about my life–my struggles, my survival, and my triumph in America–with the hope that some other young woman like myself might learn something from my story. But I was always busy; there never seemed to be a good time to write it. The thought of writing a book was even overwhelming, I thought to myself, where will I even begin? Lately, many friends, especially A.B. and my husband, have told me that I should write this book. Even though I have many things keeping me busy, including my eleven-year-old son, I thought to myself, there may never be a "right time." So, one hot summer day, as I sat in an air-conditioned and cool room, I decided it was time.

I hired a book-writing consultant. I remember my first appointment; as I shared the story of my life in Nigeria, coming to America, and my struggle to make it, I realized writing this book would bring back all my painful memories. As I sat there crying, I began to have second thoughts about writing my story. I asked myself what I was trying to accomplish by writing this book. After all, I now have a comfortable income and a happy family life, but then I thought about the many young women out there who need the encouragement to persevere and turn their dreams into realities, *no matter what life hands them.*

This book touches on the issues facing most women all over the world. It addresses bullying at every age from childhood through adulthood, the struggle to get an education, dating, and racism in corporate America. The book also addresses one woman's determination to succeed in life no matter what. Finally, this book is about having the hope, strength, and courage to make your dreams a reality.

Preface
Does this Sound Like You?

- Do you ever think to yourself "I feel like a failure" and you just can't find the motivation to get where you know you can go in life, no matter what you do, you end up in the same place...empty...frustrated... and you don't know what to do about it?

- Are you uncertain about how to create a life you want?

- Do you find yourself unable to move forward in life to accomplish your dream?

- Do you feel stuck because you are not making enough money to pay your bills and live a comfortable life?

- Are you struggling to find a job you have passion about?

- Do you need help overcoming low self-esteem and poverty?

- Do you require assistance in moving on, separating yourself from abusive, toxic, and jealous friends?

In this book, you will learn how I moved on from a humble and impoverished beginning, got an education, and prospered in the face of adversity, racism, and without family or financial support. You will discover how I created the life I wanted and realize how important it is to have the highest level of education possible.

You will learn to overcome the challenge of envious and jealous friends. You will find out how to get out of toxic relationships and become more assertive. At the same time, you will also see the importance of taking time to develop solid and supportive friendships, because it really is lonely when you get to the top.

You will learn how to deal with your wounded inner child who wants to be liked and seeks approval from others. In other words, you will learn how to overcome your past.

The intention of this book is to give you the courage and the hope to create a life you want and also to assure you that whatever you want in life is within your reach. If you trust your inner self and focus on your desired goals, you will find the strength inside of you that you haven't recognized has always been there. As you read through the chapters, you will see the will and desire to survive and the natural instincts to move through the challenges that life throws at you, the highs and the frustrations that can cause you to want to quit along the way, and the gift of strength when you don't.

If Tami can make things happen in her life, you can, too!

There are "Reflection" sections at the beginning of each chapter, and "Exercises and Lessons Learned" at the end of each chapter that you can work through and apply to your life.

Let's get started on what I hope is an exciting journey and the beginning of making the life of your dreams your reality.

Chapter 1

Growing Up Abandoned

Reflections

When you reflect upon your childhood, it may bring back negative and sad feelings just as I felt when I started writing this book. Maybe you felt helpless because of what was happening to you, and you didn't have a way to control what was happening. For example, I couldn't control when my father left to go to America or when my mother left to go back to Benin. At the same time, think about something that was positive in your childhood. For me, I had my grandmother who I knew loved me and would protect me. For you, this could be your childhood friend, your grandmother, your teacher, or your pastor who protected you and gave you comfort. Your self-esteem as a child was dependent upon so many people and situations outside of your control. But now you're an adult. You have choices and you make the decisions.

I remember being a little girl in a tiny village called Ijofin. Ijofin was in Nigeria, had a small population, no running water or electricity, and dirty streets. Unless you were from a wealthy family, people lived in a hut. Five or more people slept in one room, and most houses were made of clay cement. My family was neither poor nor wealthy; we were in-between.

My childhood memories are vague and begin when I was maybe seven or eight years old. I felt insecure, like I did not belong anywhere or to anyone. I remember walking around in no particular direction—walking around barefoot on dirty, narrow streets surrounded by a lot of green trees. When I got sick, I had no one to hold me and tell me everything was going to be okay. I remember only one time when my mother held me. I had the flu or a cold and was shaking badly. After she held me for a while, I stopped shaking. It felt good to be held; I felt calm, secure, and loved.

My father left Nigeria to go to America when I was very young. Growing up, I heard different things about him, but I did not remember what he looked like. I saw various pictures of him and his new family from Chicago that he would send to my grandmother. I only knew him through the pictures and what other people told me about him. My father was an educated and very smart man. When he left for America, he was going to get a job and a place to stay and then send for my mother, me, my sister, and my brother. But this was not what happened.

My mother waited for my father to send for her to come to America for a few years, but then she moved back to her hometown in Benin, which is in a different part of Africa. She remarried and had one son. I often wonder why she did not take her children with her when she left. I was told that when she left to go back to her hometown, she could not take her children with her because in Africa the children automatically belong to the father and his family when they get divorce or separated. Therefore, when she left, she left me and my sister behind.

At that time, I felt abandoned and alone.

My mother was a sweet and pleasant person. Everybody liked her. She did not like conflict or confrontation. My mother's philosophy has always been, "go along to get along." Unfortunately, she passed away in July of 2007. When I went home for her funeral, I was picked up at the airport by my two cousins. The first thing they asked me for was the money that I had brought with me. As I sat in the car, and as my cousin drove through the crowd on unpaved roads filled with potholes, all of sudden I started crying and could not stop. I was thinking to myself that my mother—who was always there and with me in spirit— had never asked me for money or pressured me for anything. She was the only one who was always truly happy to see me whenever I went back to Nigeria to visit. She was always grateful for whatever I sent to her from America; now she was gone.

After my father and mother left, my sister stayed with our aunt, our father's older sister Shifau as her helper, and I stayed with my grandmother Asanat for a while. I loved my grandmother. She was so kind and protective, always protecting us from my other aunts who did not treat us well. One of my aunts who lived close to my grandmother always wanted me to wash all of her entire family's clothes (12 people), which I had to do by hand. First, I had to collect water from wells into a large pan, then I washed the clothes with soap and water; and finally hung them to dry on a rope. I had to do this for twelve hours almost every weekend. It was only later when I came to United States that I discovered that a washer and dryer could do this task without me physically exhausting myself all weekend.

The only great childhood memories I have are playing outside in the dirty sand with other children in the warm breezy weather, particularly with my grandmother's young helper, Abeni. Abeni was my age, her father had sent her to live with my grandmother as her helper. She helped her do errands; she was to stay with my grandmother until she got married. Even at her young age, Abeni's father had taught Abeni her place in society. She knew the plans for her life, which did not include getting an education. The difference between me and Abeni was that I did not have a plan. I didn't even know the meaning of a life plan.

Abeni lived with my grandmother until she was about sixteen years of age and never had any schooling. Her father then sent her to Mecca; she became Alhaja. Mecca is a city in western Saudi Arabia considered by Muslims to be the holiest city of Islam. Mecca is the birthplace of the prophet Muhammad; it was the scene of his early teachings before his emigration to Medina. On Muhammad's return to Mecca, it became the center of the new Muslim faith. Alhaja is used as a title for Muslims who have been to Mecca as a pilgrim. After Abeni became Alhaja, she later married and had several children. I am not sure how many. Abeni was my best childhood friend and we did not keep in touch when I left for America. I missed Abeni's friendship.

My grandmother Asanat did the best she could for me when she was around. She was a businesswoman and was busy most of the time. My grandmother was in the clothing, tie-dye business. She tie dyed beautiful dresses. Abeni and I helped her sell them at the market.

When I started elementary school in Ijofin, my grandmother fed me breakfast, and I walked three or four miles with other neighborhood children to school. Sometimes, I walked home alone. Whenever I walked home alone, I was always afraid that I was going to be kidnapped on my way to or from school, since kidnapping young girls was very common back then in 1974. After school, I was on my own to take care of myself until evening, when my grandmother came home. Abeni went to market during the day; in the evening, she helped prepare dinner. After dinner, Abeni and I played for a little while and then went to bed; this routine started all over again the next morning.

When I was about ten years old, I was sent to stay with my other aunt in another small village called Ipokia. I called my aunt "Mama Ipokia." Mama Ipokia was very social. She liked to attend different events. Sometimes, she would take me, and she always made sure I had a plate of food to eat. Mama Ipokia was one of five wives of her husband. They all shared the same house, but each woman had her own room with a bed and space for one person. Every night, I laid down a mat and slept on the floor right outside my aunt's door. Mama Ipokia was not educated, she never attended school, but she was passionate about young children getting an education. She made sure that I went to school, and she passed along to me her deep beliefs about the importance of getting an education. When I was not in school, I helped her with her business and ran errands for her.

I developed my entrepreneurial spirit from my grandmother and Mama Ipokia. She was a businesswoman as well. The year she went to Mecca, she instructed me to buy a big bag of salt. I put the salt in smaller sandwich bags, sealed them with a flame, and then went around the neighborhood and market to sell them. Mama Ipokia was gone for thirty days. I was supposed to sell the salt, make a profit, and have that money waiting for her when she returned from Mecca, but I was sick for most of that time. I did not sell much salt; I made very little Naira instead of the thousands of Naira that I had been expected to make. Mama Ipokia was extremely upset when she came back to find out that I had made very little money while she was gone.

While living with Mama Ipokia, in my last year in elementary school, I noticed all my classmates were interviewing to enter high school. You had to be interviewed to be accepted into high school, but all the interview questions were in English. I could not speak English. I did not know anyone of influence to speak on my behalf, so I was not accepted into any high school. The elementary school system was very different in Nigeria than it is here in America; I do not remember having any structure or support system for learning, but I do remember, at the end of each year, all the students gathered outside the school building to see their grades. If you received a grade of D or F, you got in a line, held out your hand, and got whipped or beaten with a stick. I ended up on this line many times, and afterward, I had open blisters all over my hand, which were very painful.

After I did not get accepted into any high school in any nearby village, I thought my education was over. But then I received the good news that a high school was being built back in my hometown, Ijofin, and you didn't need to have an interview for you to be admitted. You just had to be a resident of Ijofin. My aunt sent me back to live with my grandmother in Ijofin so I could attend high school there. I struggled my first year in high school because there was no one at home to help me with my homework. My grandmother did not have a formal education nor speak English, so she could not help me. At the end of the year, my grades were not the best.

Sometimes, my grandmother commented that she had received a few offers for me to enter into an arranged marriage from families with sons from all over the village, which is common in Africa. She mentioned that if my father did not send for me to come to America to join him one day, she could choose a perfect husband for me.

One afternoon in June of 1980 when I was fifteen years old and at the end of my first year in high school, I came home to find my uncle Sabitu visiting from Lagos. He informed me that my father had sent for me, my brother Olu, and my sister Risi. I was so happy we were going to America, the country of endless opportunities, where everything was so easy, or so I thought. I had heard so many things about America. Some family members were excited for us; others were jealous that we were going to America and they were not. Everyone came to say their farewells and give us gifts, and we left for the airport in Lagos.

However, there was an issue with our passports, and we did not leave Lagos until August of 1980. We stayed with my uncle who lived in Lagos during the months of June, July, and August as we waited for the passport issue to be resolved. I dreamt almost every night that I was the size of a fly, trying to climb a huge and infinite mountain. I would wake up very scared. At the time, I had no idea what those dreams meant; looking back now, I know they were about what was to come, the struggles and obstacles that lay ahead. Finally, on August 8, the passport issues were resolved. It was time for us to leave, and I was very happy when the plane took off, thinking I was finally going to have a good and easy life.

Exercise

In this exercise, look back at your own childhood and answer the following questions:

1. Who protected you as a child?

_____

_____

2. Whose love and support did you count on?

_____

_____

3. Who and what made you happy as a child?

_____

_____

4. As a child, did you ever feel abandoned and alone? When?

_____

_____

5. Did you ever feel as a child that you didn't fit in with your family or felt outside of your family?

_____

_____

6. If you could relive your childhood and teenage years again, what would you do differently?

_____

_____

7. What words would describe your childhood? Write them in the lines below.

_____

_____

8. What can you do now to move past and overcome your childhood hurts and trauma to live a rewarding life?

_____

_____

Lessons Learned

- I learned to have faith and pray to God.

- I learned to dream and hope when there was no evidence that my dreams and hopes would come true.

- I learned to continue to dream and hope in the face of delays and problems.

- I learned to adapt to different environments and different conditions.

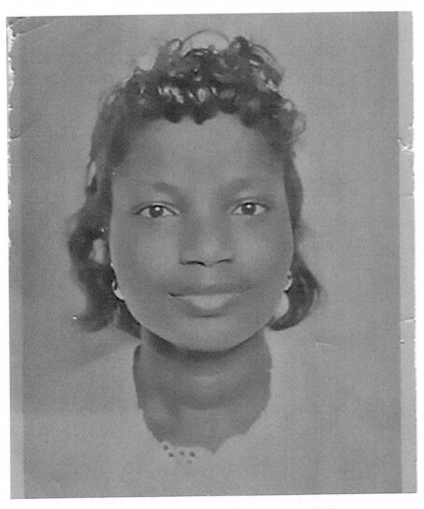

Figure 1. Tami at a young age growing up in Ijofin.

Figure 2. Lagos.

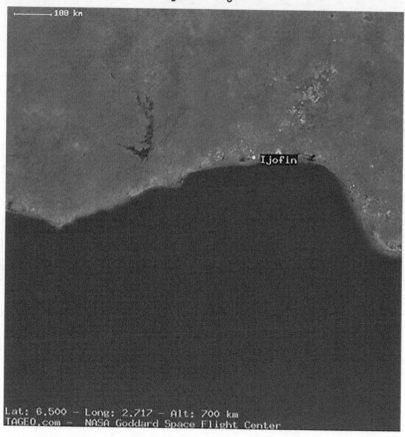

Figure 3. Ijofin Village, Africa. This is where I was born in 1965.

Figure 4. Lagos

Figure 5. Tami's mother Anura.

Figure 6. Tami's sister Risi and her brother Olu. Chicago, 1982.

Chapter 2

Coming to America

Reflections

When you think that your dreams are slowly becoming nightmares, think about your goals and continue to believe and hope. As Joel Osteen always says, you have choices in life; you can choose to be the victim or the victor. You can choose to keep your dreams in front of you and not be distracted. Joel Osteen is an American preacher, televangelist, author, and the pastor of Lakewood Church, the largest Protestant church in the United State in Houston, Texas.

On August 18, 1980, we arrived at the Lagos airport. The airport was very chaotic, full of different people, a swarm of men urging us to let them help us with our luggage for a fee. It didn't matter; I was excited at the prospect of finally coming to America. Most of our family came to the airport to see us off. My mother and four of my cousins were there; my mother had come a few days before to say her good-byes. I looked over at my brother and my sister —they were smiling and happy; we were off to the land of beauty and opportunity.

We said good-bye as they called for us to get onto the plane. My mother was crying, but my brother, sister, and I were smiling as we boarded. It was the first time I had ever been on a plane; it was scary and exciting at the same time. Thirty minutes after the plane took off, we were served dinner. After dinner, I looked around me; everyone was sleeping, I was so excited I couldn't sleep. At the time, I did not have a watch, but the travel time from Africa to London and then to Chicago took a long time.

Finally, we heard the airline pilot announce we would be landing in Chicago in fifteen minutes. I looked out the window and saw the most beautiful skyline I had ever seen. I kept saying, "Wow! Wow! Wow! What a sight to see." It was amazing. I was even more excited than I had been before we left Nigeria. We landed at O'Hare airport and an airline stewardess told my brother, sister, and me to wait by the door. We did not have any luggage to pick up, anyway.

When everybody was off the plane, the stewardess took us to an office where we were met by my father. When I saw my father, I realized I didn't have an urge to rush and hug him, probably because I really did not know him; he was like a stranger to me. I looked at him as he spoke to a group of men, checking to see if he looked the same as he did in the pictures. I did not remember ever seeing him before; it was if I met my father for the very first time at age fifteen.

My father and the men conversed for an hour or so. I had no idea what they were talking about. I could neither speak nor understand an ounce of English, except for the words "yes" and "no."

Finally, my father walked over to where we were sitting. He said, "Okay, we can go home now."

I thought to myself, "We will finally live with my father as a family.

Then my father asked where our luggage was. We told him that our uncle, his brother, told us we were not supposed to bring any clothes or luggage.

My father responded, "That is not correct. I told him not to let you bring too much luggage because otherwise you might be deported right away from the airport."

All we had were the clothes we were wearing. I was still excited, though I was starving; we had not eaten for hours.

I was still saying to myself, "We are going to finally meet his family in Chicago and we will all live together as a family."

At that time, I wished my mother was there with us, but I knew she had made her peace with the fact that she had remarried in Africa and was not coming to America.

The Kennedy expressway was so clean compared to the dirty roads in Nigeria. I looked at all the nice houses, apartments, and townhomes along the expressway.

I said to myself, "I would like to live in one of those one day."

Finally, we arrived at a house where I thought I would meet my other sisters, my stepmother, and her children from her previous marriage.

Instead, we arrived at a dark house where no one was there.

I thought, "Where are we? Where is my father's wife; where are my other sisters, Fausat and Basira?"

Then my father said, "Here, I have dinner for you."

I told myself to forget all those questions; I was starving and had to eat.

We finished eating and my father said to me, "Olu and I will be going to my house now. You and your sister, Risi, will stay here with your cousin, Bashiru."

Confused, I asked, "Why can't we live with you?

He said, "All of us cannot live together because my house is not big enough."

There was no room for my sister and me to live with him and his new family. He took us upstairs to show us where our bedroom was supposed to be, then left with my brother. This was not part of my big dream in America, but I was still hopeful.

My sister and I looked at each other and said, "Now what?" We didn't have pajamas to wear, but we had toothpaste and a toothbrush with us, so we brushed our teeth and went to bed in our underclothes.

The next morning, August 21, 1980, was a sunny and crisp day. We got up, brushed our teeth, showered, and put on the same outfits we had worn from Africa. In the bathroom, I noticed the showerhead above with hot water coming down. Where I was living in Nigeria, there was no such thing; if we wanted to take a hot shower, we had to boil the water using a pail and scoop to take the shower.

I missed all my clothes and belongings I left in Nigeria, especially the beautiful outfits my relatives had given us as parting gifts. Later that day, my father brought over some old clothes from my stepmother. They really didn't fit, but I had no choice. I was just grateful to have different outfits to wear.

My sister and I ate breakfast and then sat by the window in our room, which faced the street. We watched people as they went by and could not believe we were in America. We still had not seen our host cousin, Bashiru, who we were supposed to be staying with.

Bashiru drove a taxicab and mostly worked through the night. He came in very early and went to sleep before we woke up. One morning, once my sister and I got up and dressed, he greeted us. We finally were seeing each other again after so many years. Bashiru gave my sister and me $5 to go to a Burger King restaurant that was not too far from the house, and he wanted us to stay there for a while. He was disappointed when we came back too soon because he was entertaining his lady friend. My feeling at the time was that my cousin Bashiru did not want us living with him; he did not want us there because he was a bachelor who enjoyed living alone.

Exercise

In this exercise, look into your own life. Think about when you felt unwanted.

Also think about how you felt when what you had dreamed of for so long didn't turn out as you expected.

1. When did you feel like something you had dreamed of for so long did not happen as you expected?

   _____

   _____

2. When in your life did you feel unwanted or abandoned?

   _____

   _____

3. When have you felt alone?

   _____

   _____

4. If you still feel abandoned and alone, who can you talk to, or where can you get help?

_____

_____

Lessons Learned

- I learned to still believe in my dreams even though things that were happening were not what I had imagined.

- I learned to keep a positive attitude when all my hopes and dreams were falling apart one by one.

Figure 7. Tami, at age twenty-five, returned to visit Nigeria in 1990.

Figure 8. Map of Chicago.

Figure 9. View of the Chicago skyline.

25

Chapter 3

The Beginning of the Struggle

Reflections

Young people as well as adults will tear each other down with unkind words and do everything in their power to undermine the other person's confidence level. I am a strong believer that what happens to us as children has an enormous impact on our lives as adults. But as an adult, you have the choice to heal through coaching or counseling. It does not matter what you went through as a child; you are not alone, do not be ashamed. Always forgive those who have done you wrong because not forgiving them is probably hurting you more, and it is really beside the point whether or not the people who hurt you should have known better. When you think about how you were humiliated, neglected, or abused, remember that it is not your fault. You cannot control other people's actions. You need to learn to move forward in life sometimes through the help of professionals.

We continued to stay with my cousin; my father would come pick us up when he could. He taught us to take buses from my cousin's house to his house and to the school we would be attending in the fall. One Saturday afternoon, my father took us to a flea market to get some outfits to wear to school. Most of the outfits we saw there were for older people, most of the clothing styles were outdated, but I did not have any say in this decision. My sister was the lucky one; we could not find her clothing size at the flea market, so my father took her to Venture Store to buy her outfits. Her clothes were brand new, and they fit. We kept the same yellow shoes we wore from Nigeria.

At the end of August, school started. I had to repeat my freshman year of high school because I could not speak English, so I started as a freshman at John Marshal High School. The first day, and on many days to follow, the other kids made fun of my clothes and my Afro hairstyle as I walked down the hall to my classes.

They made comments like, "Where did you get those clothes, from your grandmother's closet?" or "You don't know how to dress in America" or "Your sweater does not match your pants" and "Your shoes do not match your clothes."

These comments went on and on, continuing through my high school years, and finally became less frequent when I was a senior. I would go to the bathroom and cry. I did not have any friends, mainly because if you are not "cool" or dress cool, nobody wants to be your friend. I could not wait until my last class period so I could go home and not have to see these students until the next day. This is when I found out how cruel high school students could be.

One Saturday afternoon, my father came over to my cousin's house. He argued with my cousin. I didn't hear the whole conversation, but after the argument, my cousin said to me that he was renting the house from my father, and we were living there while he was still paying full rent. The next thing we knew, my father told my sister and me that we were moving to the basement. For a while, we lived and slept in an unfinished, concrete basement. I would have a bad day at school and then come home to a freezing basement. This was not what I thought my life in America would be. I wished my mother was there to comfort me. Most nights, I cried until I fell asleep.

Before I fell asleep, I always thought to myself, "I know that another kind of life is possible." I would imagine that I was living in a nice and warm home surrounded by loving family. Then I would say to myself, "I will need an education to get a good job so I will be able to afford to live in a nice place."

For the rest of my freshman year, every morning around 6:00 a.m., my father picked us up and took us to his house, which was about twenty minutes away. Then he would go to work. We waited at his house until it was time to go to school. Then we would walk to school. In the afternoon, my sister and I would take the bus back to my cousin's house.

Then the winter weather came, and that year was the coldest year of my life. I had no coat to wear. I had a jacket that was more like a shirt, not warm at all. I did not have a hat or gloves, and I did not have a book bag. I carried my books in my hands. By the time I got to school in the morning, I could not feel my toes and fingers. Also, since I did not have an umbrella, when it rained, I would be soaking wet when I got to school. Every morning as I walked to school, I saw my classmates on the bus laughing and pointing at me. Thankfully, I could not hear what they were saying, but I knew they were making fun of me. Eventually, one of my teachers, Mrs. Dixon, felt sorry for me; she helped me get a discounted bus pass. I was very grateful to her because I did not have to walk to school in the cold and rain anymore; I could take a warm, dry bus.

Things got even worse when it snowed because I didn't have snow boots to wear, either. The first time I saw snow, it looked amazing. My sister and I got up one morning, looked outside, and there were white salt-like flakes everywhere. We had never seen or heard of snow. My sister and I went outside to taste it because we thought it was salt, but we quickly discovered that it was not.

In high school, with all the cruel comments, constant discomfort, and lack of friends, I was barely passing my classes. In December of that year, my father registered me for a Certified Nursing Assistant's (CNA) program in downtown Chicago. I took the train every Saturday for the six-month program, which I passed to become a CNA. I was happy as my freshman year came to an end. It meant I would not be teased by the other students for a while.

At the end of that summer, my father found another place for my sister and me to live. Mrs. Smith, his babysitter's friend, lived in a three-bedroom house and had one daughter, Rona. Rona was away in college when we first moved in with Mrs. Smith. My sister and I moved into the one bedroom in Mrs. Smith's house that had a couch that pulled out into a bed. We paid $200 per month rent. I was happy; this meant no more sleeping in the cold basement. We finally had a warm room.

Rona later became like a sister to me. Although we did not see or talk to each other often, I knew she was always there for me when I needed her, and I was there whenever she needed me. Rona is extremely kind-hearted. (I was very grateful to her when she offered to stay with me after I had surgery one year.)

During that same summer, my father also took me and my recently awarded CNA certificate to a nursing home in Oak Lawn called Manor-Care Skilled Nursing Facility. I filled out a job application and got hired the same day; I would be earning $3.75 per hour. Every two weeks when I get my check, I gave it to my father. He taught me how to take the bus to work on my own. This worked for a while until I went back to school in the fall and worked after school from 3 p.m. to 11:30 p.m. My father had to pick me up at 11:30 p.m. because the bus did not run that late. Every night after work, my father brought me a Big Mac and a Coke from McDonald's. I wished so badly that my father just would have given me the money to buy dinner during my dinner break instead of bringing me food at 11:30 p.m. Sometimes, one of my coworkers, Mary, would buy me dinner. Mary was kind and generous to pay for my food when I did not have the money.

I never had money; whenever I got my check, I gave it to my father. He told me he was putting it in the bank, and he used some of the money for our rent. He would give my sister and me $20 to spend for the whole week. I was happy when our neighbor asked me to iron clothes for her on the weekends; this gave me extra cash to buy the necessities that my sister and I could not buy with the $20 my father gave us.

I worked as a CNA that whole summer until I went back to school in the fall. I didn't know what it meant to have fun. I didn't go anywhere or do anything that was fun. Once in a while, I would go to the movies with Rona. I was not dating anyone, and I did not have any real friends.

Exercise

Think back in your life to when you felt humiliated, to that painful period when you did not have anyone there to support or comfort you. Why do you think you were teased? Actually, it doesn't really matter why; the point is you were, and how did it make you feel?

1. When were you teased or gossiped about?

_____

_____

2. Do you think you were teased because you were different?

_____

_____

3. Do you think you were teased because you didn't fit in?

_____

_____

4. Do you think you were teased because you dressed differently?

_____

_____

5. Do you think you were teased because you were not popular?

_____

_____

6. Who helped you in your time of need? Have you thanked him or her recently?

_____

_____

Lessons Learned

- I learned to make the most of my situation.

- I learned to focus on my education regardless of other students teasing me and making fun of my clothes.

- I learned not to let the horrible comments my high school class-mates made bother me and didn't let them prevent me from going to school even when I was terribly embarrassed and ashamed.

- I learned to believe that things happen for a reason that we don't fully understand as they are happening.

Chapter 4

Education: A Ladder out of the Basement

Reflections

It is easy to give up on your dreams as you face obstacles, but don't get distracted. Remember the expression: when one door closes, another opens. I am a strong believer that if there is a will, there is a way. Just when you feel as if things could not get any worse, they do, but you cannot give up. When you run into obstacles, you must look for ways to turn them into opportunities. You must find the strength within you, focus on your desired goals, keep taking actions, reevaluate your failures and take responsibility for them, and hang in until the end. It is only those people who have the passion, the desire, and are serious about achieving their goals who hang in until the end and revel in their success.

For the rest of my high school years, I went to school during the day and worked as a Certified Nursing Assistance (CNA) in the evening. I took a bus from school to work and did my homework during my break and dinnertime. My father picked me up at 11:30 p.m. until I was able to buy a used 1976 Firebird, my first car.

Working as a CNA was very challenging. It is physically demanding; you are on your feet most of the day helping the residents living in the nursing home who are not able to help themselves. Luckily, I had the opportunity to work with a great group of caring CNAs. We worked as a team; we always worked in groups, and everyone in the group was a great worker.

At the beginning of the shift, the outgoing CNAs gave us reports about all the residents. We loaded the cart with bed linens, towels, wash towels, soaps, and so on and just went from room to room and took care of the residents. I first learned to work as part of a team at this job. I loved how we all worked together and helped one another. Most of the other CNAs were my age and some were older.

The only friend I made in high school was Mrs. Dixon, my teacher. She was known to be a very tough teacher, but to me she was the kindest and most generous person I have ever known. She invited me to eat lunch in her office because I always ate lunch by myself in the cafeteria since no other students would invite me to sit or eat with them, and I was too afraid to go and sit with them without an invitation.

I did not attend homecoming, but thanks to Mrs. Dixon and Mrs. Smith, I was able to attend my high school prom. Mrs. Dixon asked another senior student if he would go to the prom with me. Mrs. Smith paid to have my prom dress made, and it was a nice experience to be able to go to the prom. Mrs. Dixon helped me through my darkest days in high school. High school was a dark time in my life: I did not have much support in school or any at home, I was made fun of most of the day, and I did not speak English. I felt sad all the time. I can never repay Mrs. Dixon for her help and support during this time; I still keep in touch with her today.

In my senior year of high school, I had a falling out with my father. It started when I needed money to get my hair done. I asked my father for an extra $20 that week, and for some reason that I could not understand, he refused. I got upset and refused to give him my paychecks after that incident. Since I would not give him my checks, he placed a lock on my car. But I still found a way to go to school and work without my car. I took a bus to work in the afternoon and then would beg for a ride to any bus stop after work to take the bus home.

In time, I learned to forgive my father. These days, I am very grateful to my father for bringing me, my brother, and my sister to America. We had opportunities that we would not have had if we were still in Nigeria; we had an opportunity to get an education. If not for my education, I probably would not be where I am today or have accomplished what I have personally and professionally. I believe my father did the best he could when he brought us to America. When he left Nigeria to come to America, I believe he had the best intentions. He did what he had to do, and I made a promise to myself to do what I have to do to make my dreams come true; I cannot use what happened to me as an excuse.

I was happy to graduate from high school. Mr. Smith, Mrs. Smith, Rona, and my sister Risi were at my graduation ceremony. I was not aware that I should have already picked out a college, applied, and been accepted by the time I graduated. I continued to work as a CNA at the nursing home the summer after graduation. They always needed CNAs, so I worked a lot of overtime. I worked sixty to seventy hours per week to save for college. I did not have a social life. I worked sixteen hours every Saturday and Sunday.

Since I had no idea I was supposed to be researching, visiting colleges, and selecting them during my junior and senior years in high school, that summer after I graduated, I researched a few city colleges. My father had always told me to say "nursing" when people asked what I wanted for my major in college, though I had no idea what nurses did. From my research, I found Olive Harvey College and started to take prerequisites for the nursing program. I was not qualified for financial aid because I was not a US citizen, and my father was not able to assist with college tuition. But I was lucky; the school let me pay for my classes in monthly installments. I took classes through the fall, winter, spring, and summer, and received As and Bs in all my classes. I went to school during the day and worked in the evening. Soon, I was done with all the prerequisites for nursing and needed to apply for the actual nursing program. I wanted to get my bachelor's degree rather than an associate's, so I applied to the University of Illinois at Chicago (UIC).

I was accepted and I started taking nursing classes. UIC's tuition was much higher than that at Olive Harvey College. The classes were bigger, and the courses were harder. I had to continue to work many jobs to pay the tuition. I was tired all the time and not able to study. I fell asleep in classes and started getting Ds and Fs. At the end of that year, I was expelled.

That was the worst summer I have ever had. I cried and cried. This meant the end of my education, and I had wanted to accomplish so much more! One day, I received a recruitment postcard for nursing students from Trinity Christian College in Palos Heights. I felt like I had won the lottery–and a second chance. This was a blessing from God. Before I went to work the next day, I went to Trinity College to talk to someone about enrolling in the nursing program. The college was fifteen to twenty minutes from Manorcare Skilled Nursing and Rehab, where I worked as a CNA. The class size was very small, about twenty-two people. I learn much better in smaller classes. I was able to start their nursing program in 1987; I made new friends and I was getting As and Bs in all my classes. In June of 1990, I received my Bachelor of Science in Nursing.

With working a lot of hours, doing homework, and studying for school, I was not able to help Mrs. Smith with housework and other chores; she was not happy with me. Two years before I graduated from nursing school, Mrs. Smith, from whom I was renting a room, informed me I had to move out within a month. On my CNA salary, I was not able to afford a decent apartment on my own. Mrs. Smith referred me to her friend who had an extra room for rent. I went to see the room; it was nice and clean, so I took it. My first night there was scary; I woke up in the middle of the night to go to the bathroom, and as I put the light on, I got up and saw all these cockroaches running away from the bed. When I got to the bathroom, I put the light on and saw a lot more cockroaches running all over the floor. After two months in this place, I knew I had to move out.

I was referred to another place that was available for rent at $250 per month; it was a basement apartment. On a CNA salary, that was all I could afford. It was located in a nice area of Chicago called Beverly, and it was a lovely place to live.

However, my landlord was very involved in and picky about everything I did, from what I cleaned with to where I hung my clothes in my room. She told me she had a problem with me when she saw a towel on the floor in the bathroom. When I stepped out of the shower, the bathroom floor was always cold, so I placed towels on the floor to step on because I could not afford to buy a bathroom rug. My landlord even came in and out of my place when I was not there.

One weekend I was cleaning the place, and she ran down to tell me that she could smell what I was cleaning with upstairs, and she did not like it, and I needed to buy different cleaning supplies without chemicals. I told her I could only buy what I could afford. A month later, she informed me she was giving me a week to move out.

At that time, I was studying for my finals; I was stressed and didn't know what to do. One of my coworkers, Lucy, offered me her basement to stay in. Her husband made a bedroom, kitchen, and a bathroom with a shower in their basement; I was comfortable. Lucy and her husband had three children and were a very nice family. Lucy was very kind to me. I was able to stay there until I finished college and could afford to purchase a house of my own. Lucy and I became friends. When I had my son, she was a big help to me; she would keep my son over the weekend or when I had to go out of town.

As I wrote this chapter, I thought about Lucy, and I called her. I told her how much I had appreciated that she took me in when I didn't have anywhere else to go and was afraid I was going to become homeless.

She answered me, "I said to myself, this girl is so young and working so hard, I have to do something to help her."

I ended up staying with Lucy and her family for a few years. After I graduated from nursing school, I was able to get a mortgage to buy my own home with two bedrooms and a full basement. It was small, but I loved it. Now a registered nurse, I continued to work part time at Manorcare as a PM Supervisor and full-time job at a hospital. I also went on to go to graduate school where I received my Master of Science in Nursing (MSN) and Master of Business Administration (MBA). After I worked and saved for a few years, I was able to buy a beautiful high-rise condo in downtown Chicago overlooking Millennium Park.

Exercise

1. In this exercise, think about when you kept running into obstacle after obstacle in your life as you pursued your dreams. Think about how you were able to turn these obstacles into opportunities.

   _____

   _____

2. When and where in your life did you feel like you wanted to give up on your goals and dreams?

   _____

   _____

3. Who are the people who encouraged and helped you? Have you thanked those people recently?

   _____

   _____

4. What made you continue to hope and take steps toward your goals and dreams?

   _____

   _____

Lessons Learned

- I learned not to be distracted from my goal of getting an education.

- I learned to take the good with the bad.

- I learned that God does not abandon us when we need him the most and to have faith.

- I learned to do whatever I needed to do, such as working two or three jobs, to make the money to pay for my education.

- I learned to stay focused to achieve my goals.

- I learn to let go of any cruel words that were spoken to me when I was younger. I am worthy of kindness.

- I learned to work through my painful history and let it go.

Figure 10. Tami's graduation picture as Certified Nurse's Assistant (CNA).

Figure 11. Tami's high school graduation day in 1984.

Figure 12. Tami's junior year high school picture.

Figure 13. Happy to be graduating from High School.

Figure 14. Tami's graduation day from Graduate School in 1995, receiving her Master of Science in Nursing (MSN) degree.

Chapter 5
The Truth about Friendships

Reflections

As a woman, always trust and follow your instincts about people. When you feel very uncomfortable about someone, and he or she makes you feel bad more times than he or she makes you feel good, it is best to keep your distance. Wouldn't it be wonderful to have another woman be genuinely happy for you when you have success in life? I believe that it is human nature for many women to be jealous and filled with envy, but they will pretend and have you believe that they are happy for you. Sometimes, you think some people are your friends, but then you start to notice how what they say undermines you, brings up all the negative aspects of your accomplishments, and magnifies your mistakes. Surprisingly, these people may be your family members and "best friends." If you have someone unhealthy in your life, it is up to you to set boundaries. You are no longer a victim, you are the victor, and you are in control.

It is never too late to try to be a good friend, they say, although when you know better, you do better. You cannot control the behavior of another woman, but you can control your reaction to the undermining and backstabbing of a jealous friend.

As I mentioned before, choose your friends carefully and ask yourself, is this person someone who tends to gossip about other women who have more of "whatever" she wants? To your face, she may be supportive, but watch your back.

If she gossips to you about other people and tells you all the bad things she did or is doing to other people, eventually she will gossip about you to other people and do all those bad things to you as well! Believe me; it has happened to me many times. I used to have a friend who would tell me that when she was upset with someone, and that when that person called on the phone and she accidentally picked up the receiver, she would pretend that she couldn't hear. She would never return their calls, and she played games with them. Well, she did the same thing to me when we had a disagreement; it hurt deeply that someone you cared about could treat you that way.

I also have personally experienced the downside of sharing your personal life at work with the entire office. The women in the office may pretend to be your friends but then they will rake you over the coals when you're not around. Again, I can't stress this enough. Consider your working world as a stage; I learned this from a Disney orientation video. You come to work and step onto the stage as a professional, and no one is allowed to show his or her true face.

There is no reason for you to open yourself up to gossip and criticism by sharing your recent break-ups or divorce, how bad your husband or boyfriend is treating you, how your twenty-five-year-old son or daughter still lives at home because he or she can't keep a job, or that you bought a new Porsche or BMW with your savings. Look and act the part of a professional at work and save the personal conversations for your trusted friends during your personal time outside work

It would be wonderful to have a world where women hold hands and support each other, but unfortunately that world does not exist. So instead, you should build your own trusted team of friends and colleagues. These friends can be of any color or race, they tell you the truth, love you, support your ideas, lift you up when you're down, and can be trusted with anything you tell them. A true friend has earned your trust and is to be valued forever. They are friends through thick and thin.

There is nothing quite like having a special friend. But to have a good friend, you must be a good friend as well.

I enjoyed working as a nurse. I met many wonderful people. Some of my coworkers became my lifelong friends and family. I did things with them on the weekends and started having fun. I went on a cruise with one of my coworkers, I had the best time of my life. I had a hard time developing friendships because I was always working all the time and didn't make the time to develop good, solid friendships. I also felt that I did not belong to any race group.

I felt as if African Blacks were always judging me because they were always making statements like, "You think you are an American! You should be ashamed of yourself for losing your African culture and forgetting your native language, Yoruba!" They were always talking behind my back. I felt that I was not fully accepted by American Blacks, either. They never let me forget that I came from Africa. They made comments like, "You are still a foreigner." I did have a few great friends from different backgrounds (African Americans and Caucasians).

As I worked as a registered nurse in various places, I met many wonderful people who influenced and helped shape my life, including Christie, Stacy, Imelda, Jacqui, Annette, Marilyn, Audrey, Vanessa, Chandra, Ethel, Sherita, Brenda, and Larinda.

I met Lavanya when I was working as a CNA, and she treated me as part of her family. She invited me to all her family picnics and to her house for dinner with her family. This meant a great deal to me since I didn't have a family of my own. Then I met Seeta who also treated me as part of her family. Seeta became one of my best friends and eventually godmother to my son. Seeta is a hard worker, funny, and a loyal friend. She does not give up on friendship easily, and she taught me how to love unconditionally. I also met Ja'vonne; I liked her honesty; she always called things the way she saw them. Javonne is kind and has a good heart; I was touched when she offered to cook dinner for me when I was sick. Dian is resourceful and so generous in sharing her resources. No matter who or what you need, whether you need a hairdresser, a baby sitter, a painter, a mover, and so on, Dian has the name and number for you to help out. Janella is kind and has a good heart. Janella always told me that she knew that I am a single mother and didn't have too many family near by, she would always offer to help me out with my son when I have to work on the weekend.

Tori, Larinda , Christie, Emelda, Marilyn, and Lynn were like sisters to me. Whenever I needed support or someone to listen, I could always count on them. I don't know where I would be if I hadn't been blessed and met them. I also met a man when I was working at nursing rehab; he taught me how a woman should be treated. What I learned from him helped me choose the man who is now my husband.

I am glad to have my sister Risi; we went through a lot together growing up. Risi is sweet, and she would give you her last dollar if you needed it. If anyone deserves a happy ending, it is Risi. She has two beautiful children, Leah and Quan.

Friendships do not come easily to me as I have been backstabbed more than once by other women. I found that as women, we are often our own worst enemies. I am not proud of this, but I have done my share of undermining a friend, family member, or acquaintance as well. I know that we all need to support and encourage one another. All I can do now is move forward; we are all human; no one is perfect.

Now, I choose my friends and inner circle very carefully. I don't share all of my life with the world at large. I found that many times when I shared personal information with people who I thought were my friends that they used the information I shared in private to talk about me with other people behind my back. I remember one time when I was seeking another position within my organization, and I told one of my coworkers who I thought was a friend. I later found out that she shared it with someone else who was interested in the same position and encouraged the other woman to apply quickly for the same position before it was given to me.

You will also meet friends who will use you and treat you as if you are their chauffeur. Some of them will act as if they are more important than you. They will act as if their time is more important than yours; when you make plans to get together, they will show up one to two hours late. And some friends will use you by dumping all their problems on you. They will keep you on the phone for hours, going on and on about their problems. It was difficult; I wish I had ended those relationships sooner.

Exercise

1. Have you ever been betrayed by a friend?

   _____

   _____

2. List the ways your friends make you feel.

   _____

   _____

3. Do you have friends who make you feel bad about yourself?

   _____

   _____

4. List the names of those friends below.

   _____

   _____

5. Do you have friends who you think only try to use you? List the names of those friends below.

   _____

   _____

6. Do you have friends who only complain about everything in their lives and bring you down in the process? List the names of those friends below.

_____

_____

7. List the ways you can separate yourself from toxic and abusive friends.

_____

_____

8. Do you have people in your life that you can trust? List those people below and make sure you nurture your relationships with them.

_____

_____

Lessons Learned

- I learned that true, good friends are to be treasured. It takes time to nurture friendships, and you should not take them for granted.

- I learned to listen to my intuition. When you feel uncomfortable about your friendship with someone, it is better to stay away from that person and move on.

- I learned that it is better to be alone than to have abusive and toxic friends.

- Remember, people will do to you what you allow them to do to you; they will also make you feel how you allow them to make you feel. No one can do anything to you without your consent.

When you look at the list of potential hazards and challenges to a woman's self-esteem, it is a shame that other women are at the top of the list. Consider the following threats to a woman's confidence: media portrayal of women, men, family members, gender bias, racial bias, stereotypes, and negative self-talk. According to the book, Starting Over: Learning to Love Yourself, by Linda Ellis Eastman, women supporting women would lead to the following:

- Emotional healing

- Less tolerance for abusive relationships

- Pride in successful ventures

- Honest, healthy female relationships

- Confidence to step outside the box

- More job opportunities

- Healthier family lives

- More compassion for other women

- Collaboration rather than competition

- Building trust

- Increased self-worth and self-love

We as women need to remember the following about one another: We feel deep grief and joy; we have days when we feel like failures; we may be married, single, widowed, or divorced; we may be straight or gay; it doesn't matter. We may have been abused as children, we may be abused now as adults, and we may have few people who believe in us. These are all the more reasons we need to support and encourage one another as women.

Figure 15. Tami in 2008.

Chapter 6

The Dark Side of
Working in Corporate America

Reflections

Always remember that your workplace is like a stage, you must perform and act your part, no matter what, you must maintain your professionalism. In the workplace, you must trust carefully. Not everyone that is nice to you is your friend. Embrace the fact that you are different from everyone else. Do not compare yourself to others. Do not compete with others. Because you have flaws does not mean you are worthless. All people have flaws; they just may not be visibly noticeable. Try to be kind to others no matter how they are behaving at work; you do not know what they are going through at home or outside work. Convince yourself that you are worthy of good things and kind treatment. Do not accept abuse and mistreatment from your friends or boss. Even though your boss has all the power, she should not abuse or misuse her power. Talk about yourself in a positive way.

I once worked with the director of nursing at a Hyde Park hospital. She taught me that in order to survive in corporate America, I must be tough. I must have a tough skin and not wear my feelings on my sleeve. I learned this lesson the hard way, because when I worked at this subacute nursing facility on the north side of Chicago, I was like a fish swimming with sharks. I learned that you must go along to get along, because when you don't, you find yourself all alone with no one to back you up.

But I could not go along with mistreating any patient. I wanted to make a difference as a nurse, and I had empathy for the patients who trusted us with their care. In a hospital, acute rehab, subacute, or any health-care facility, I believe patients need to be treated as we'd like our family, friends, or even ourselves to be treated.

I remember one incident that occurred in a subacute facility when I was a director of nursing. Two diabetic patients needed to be fed. It was 9:00 a.m., and the CNA assigned to these patients sat down to eat her breakfast. I asked if all the patients had been fed, and she responded, "I have to eat first." I explained that it is dangerous for a diabetic patient not to eat for more than twelve hours, but again she responded that she had to eat her breakfast first. She had the option to eat at any time. Patients who cannot feed themselves do not have that option; they only eat when someone feeds them. Diabetic patients who have not eaten for twelve or more hours are a concern and should take priority.

As a result of this incident, I was reported to the higher administration and reprimanded for bringing up the issue. The administrator of that subacute rehab turned against me because I would not go along. All I wanted to do was the right thing for the patients. The administration did not care. They only cared about maintaining high patient numbers and not ruffling any feathers. Eventually, I transferred to another facility.

Working as an African American woman in a corporate environment is not easy. It is very difficult to advance even with a higher education. When I first started working, I heard other African Americans saying there was a lot of racism in corporate America. I did not believe them until I experienced it myself. I definitely noticed a double standard. Caucasian nurses were treated differently than African American nurses; they did not need a higher degree to become managers, directors, vice presidents, or presidents. I have seen many African American nurses with advanced degrees, including me, working in positions requiring only an associate's or a bachelor's degree.

Sometimes, it feels like managers and directors only listened to the feedback of Caucasian nurses, not the African American nurses. When we made suggestions or voiced our work-related concerns, we were viewed as angry Black women (ABW). We were told to go talk to an employee assistant program representative (EAP).

The first time I really experienced racism was when I worked with a group of Caucasian advanced-practitioner nurses on a surgical floor. I was a care facilitator/utilization reviewer; in my position, I needed to review patient's medical records to establish the severity of illness and the intensity of the service needed. Sometimes, the reason why a patient remains in the hospital is not always documented in the patient's medical record, so I would have to ask the nurse practitioners to provide more information. They would not talk to me, but they would talk to Caucasian coworkers. Their expressions were equivalent to, "How dare you ask us questions!" They would make rude comments to me that they didn't have time, and when I texted them, they didn't respond. They would talk down to me or even try to give me orders to do things for them.

One time, they reported me to my boss and tried to get me fired. The group of nurse-practitioners even circulated a petition to have me removed from the unit. Luckily at that time, I had a wonderful manager who took the time to investigate their complaints, and she even came to the unit where I worked to attend the discharge rounds and to talk to the nurse-practitioners herself. She eventually found out there was no merit to their complaints.

From my experience, I believe that racism exists in various degree in corporate America, how you are affected by racism depends on who your direct supervisor is. Some managers are able to separate the job performance from skin color. When you have the misfortune of working under a manager who is extremely racist, that is when your work life can be miserable. Racism exist on different levels, on one level, when you do your job, perform well, and work hard, you are ok, your color is overlooked. At another level, it does not matter how well you perform or how hard you work, all they see is your skin color. When you find yourself in this position, my advice is that you look for another job as quickly as possible because it will not get any better. With hard work, discipline, and persistence, you will find another job with a manager who will respect and appreciate you for your hard work, dedications, and skill, not your skin color. You will find a company that will pay you what you are worth and respect you for what you can contribute to the organization.

I experienced full-blown racism when my department was eliminated at our hospital, and we all lost our jobs. At that time, I was fortunate to get another position at the same hospital in a different department, or so I thought. We were under different management. At first, it was like a dream place to work, but after six months, the dream turned into a nightmare. It felt like we were working on a plantation, and it was like that for the next two years. We felt that management did not listen to any ideas that came from African American nurses. Changes were made when the suggestions came from Caucasian nurses, whether it was about changing an assignment, procedure, or policy. We felt that management was not interested in hearing our side when we were reported by Caucasian nurses. When we were called into the office, we were already tried, judged, and convicted. Sometimes, we were just informed about the decision to make a change; they never asked for our input.

I had never worked before in a situation where everybody felt miserable and trapped in a job. The environment was very much one of backstabbing and watching your back; get them before they get you! Everyone felt they had to report each other. Instead of encouraging staff to work out their disagreements first, we were encouraged to go straight to management with any issue. The workplace felt like a funeral home; the whole office was so quiet you could hear a pin drop. The workload was horrendous, and it was easy to make mistakes. When we made a mistake, instead of offering to provide more support and education, the manager threatened to give us written reprimands and call HR. We were expected to be perfect at all times. Management was threatening, manipulative, and bullying. It was like a club; if you do not behave in certain ways, you are excluded from different committees. I remember my last evaluation at that job; I cannot even repeat some of the things that were said to me. I came out of the manager's office feeling like the worst person in the world.

After working there for almost two years, I was tired of being emotionally beaten and mentally abused. Once I was even told that our group was a low-functioning group and that management had to control every aspect of our working environment. My self-esteem was down to nothing; I felt like I was my wounded, inner child; I found myself sad all the time.

What I mean by my "wounded inner child" is that when I am being mistreated by another person, I feel like I am that abandoned, not worthy, powerless, and unwanted little girl all over again. When I am being mistreated, all the bad childhood memories come flooding back. A person with a wounded inner child is always constantly seeking approval from other people. Other symptoms include constant feelings of loneliness, isolation, and separation from everyone else. I overcame my wounded inner child by learning to speak up for myself. When I make mistakes, I learn from them and move on instead of beating myself up over them. I remind myself that I didn't do anything wrong as a child to make my father and mother leave me; they had their reasons.

To return to my story, I decided that I was not that wounded child. I knew that I was an adult, and I would not let my voice be silenced. I started speaking up for myself and others in a professional manner, and management did not like that at all. I felt like it was a club, and if you weren't going to do things their way, you couldn't play. Suddenly, I didn't get notifications about meetings and was left out of them. We were expected to behave a certain way; if we didn't, we were treated as outsiders in our own working environment. They decided to use my evaluation as a way to get back at me and to get me back in line, or so they thought.

Employees' performance evaluations were used to beat up the staff emotionally. Several staff members came out of the management's office after their evaluation reviews crying and repeating what was said during their evaluations. The comments were horrible and included statements like, "You are an angry person, and you need to go get help"; "You are in a dark place, and you need to get yourself out"; "If you don't like working here, why don't you leave and find another job?"; "If you are not going to go along with us, you can't work here"; "You have a negative aura about you," and on and on and on.

The management wanted everything to appear perfect to the other departments. One staff member was told she had better come to the holiday party even though she was sick because of how it would look if she were not there. The environment became very tense and harder to work in. The staff would tell on each other, reporting every little mistake to management.

I was determined to get out of there, but there weren't other well-paying jobs available. I thought about opening up my own business, but I didn't have enough capital to maintain it at that time. I could not afford to just quit. I prayed every day that God would help me get out of that place. I continued to search for a different position; I did not give up.

One morning, I received a long text from a friend about a position available at another hospital affiliated with the one where I was working. I jumped at the chance. Joel Olsteen says that what God has put together, no man or woman can mess up (or words to that effect). The way everything aligned was a miracle. I had worked with that friend about a decade before, and I told my husband that I thought she was my angel. When I first became a single parent, Scott helped me out a lot.

On my last day on that horrible job, I got to have my say to management. I was warned by my human resource representative that when I gave my resignation notification to my manager, she would get angry. I didn't think that would be the case, but I was wrong. She was angry in a passive aggressive way; she pretended she was okay with my resignation, but her behavior said otherwise. I attempted to meet with her to discuss my last day at that job and my starting date of my new job, but she blew me off many times.

Unfortunately, because my new job was at one of the affiliated hospitals, it was considered a transfer, and my current manger had a say about when I could start my new job. When she would not discuss with me my last day or when I could leave, I put in a Paid Time Off (PTO) for a couple of days before I had to start my new job. She did not respond for two weeks. A few days before my last day, my manager called me into the office, telling me she could not approve my PTO. I asked why. She stated that she needed me to stay and work until the day before I had to start my new job. I replied to her that I needed a few days off before I started my new job because I needed to do some things to prepare for it.

She replied, "That is not my problem," adding, "Why don't you take your time off when you start your new job?"

After that meeting, I realized this manager was as bad as everybody was saying, but she was an expert in faking how she felt except when she got behind closed doors. Out in the open and in front of other staff, she smiles and pretends she is the perfect and nicest manager in the world, but behind closed doors, she takes the mask off.

At my farewell party, she did not acknowledge or mention any contribution I had made to the department. I was shocked when she came to my desk on my last day just before the party to tell me that I needed to finish all my work before I left, and that she was requesting our last meeting at 3:00 p.m. that day. When I met with her, she asked for my keys, pager, and my ID, but because I was transferring to the sister hospital, I got to keep my ID. After she told me that was everything she had to talk to me about, I told her I had one thing to say to her: I told her that I felt she could at least acknowledge all I had done to contribute to the department. I had helped her do the schedule for all the nurses, which I took home to do on my own time sometimes, and I had worked hard to help the OR project be successful.

Her response was, "I am always disappointing you, aren't I?" She wished me well in my new position, and I wished her well in hers, and I left her office. That was the last time I ever saw her. It felt good at last to speak my mind without having to worry about how she could retaliate for what I said.

Until I actually left that job, I had not realized how working in a toxic environment could affect your health. Also, commuting on the train for three hours every day to work took its toll on me mentally as well as physically. I left the house at five o'clock in the morning to get to work and didn't return home until six o'clock in the evening. Keeping up with my family and work life was very hard, even overwhelming most of the time. I felt guilty at times that I was away from my family for so many hours. By the time I got home, had dinner with the family, and helped my son with his homework, it was time for him to go to bed. I felt bad for not spending good, quality time with him and the rest of the family.

When I was off work, I felt anxious because I knew I had to go back to work there, and my chest felt tight. On my last day at that job, as I got into the train to go home, I realized how relaxed I was becoming as the train pulled away from the Ogilvie train station. My chest loosened up, and my nerves became calm. Finally, my prayers had been answered. At the end of the day, now that I have been away from my old job for a while, I really think the management there did me a great favor. Because of them, I left that job, and I am now in a much better situation.

I spoke to two other former coworkers who also resigned from the same department after I did; ironically, their experiences were the same as mine had been when I left that job. One of them described how she felt after she left; she described feeling relieved, more relaxed. She said, "I feel like a dark cloud has been lifted from over my head." I remember feeling the same way. Like her, I missed some of the people I worked with, but I do not miss working in that toxic environment.

Exercise

In this exercise, think about your present job and what kind of environment you are working in. How do you feel about your job? Are you happy to go to work?

1. When in your profession did you feel like you were treated harshly, unprofessionally, mentally abused, etc.?

   _____

   _____

2. How can you change this situation now?

   _____

   _____

3. Do you find that women compete against one another? Does this ring true with you? That is, do you compete against other women? (Answer honestly.)

_____

_____

4. How can you handle this?

_____

_____

5. Which people undermine your belief in yourself and spread gossip about you?

_____

_____

6. How can you handle this situation?

_____

_____

7. Which people support, encourage, and lift you up at work?

_____

_____

8. Have you thanked those people lately? List those people; make sure you nurture your relationships with them.

_____

_____

9. What changes can you make in your life starting today? (These are areas of your life you have control over, for example: if you are not happy with your job right now, what actions can you take toward getting another job, like updating your resume, researching other available positions you might be interested in, etc.)

_____

_____

10. What areas of your life are you unable to change? (For example, you have no control over your height, family history, and chronic illness.)

_____

_____

Lessons Learned

- Being abused in any way is never okay, even if the person abusing you is your supervisor.

- We all have choices in life; we can choose to be victims or victors.

- I learned to remind myself that I am an adult, and I expect to be treated as such.

- I am a professional woman, and I should be treated as one.

- I learned to stop diminishing my successes to make others feel better.

- I learned to stop verbally deflating myself in front of my peers.

- I learned to be careful about whom I trust.

- I learned to always give people the benefit of the doubt and to believe the good in everybody—even after I was stabbed in the back too many times to recount. As women, we need to support each other instead of facing off against each other. It does not have to be women vs. women. Instead of supporting one another, we women tend to crush other women by undermining and spreading rumors about each other. This should stop, right now!

- I learned that a secure woman with high self-esteem does not have time to start vicious rumors; she is comfortable with herself and does not need to undermine others to make herself feel or look better.

Chapter 7

In Pursuit of Love and Happiness

Reflections

Remember that real life is not as perfect or the same as what you see on TV. To achieve your dreams, you will have to let go of that illusion. The journey and the roads you take to achieving your dreams may not look like what you think they should look like. Work hard to get what you want; eventually, it will pay off. Again, no matter what kind of obstacles you encounter, you must stay focused, never give up, and be persistent.

At this point, I had gotten out of that cold, concrete basement when I got my nursing degree, and I had saved enough money to own a cozy condo in downtown Chicago. But then I found myself without a man to share my life. Every night, I came back from work to an empty house, and what I really wanted was a home and a loving family.

I had spent so many years getting my education and finding work that once I achieved those goals, I realized I was lonely and wanted, finally, to fulfill my long-held dream of having a family. Watching all the holiday movies always depressed me. Whether in wonderful or not-so-wonderful situations, these movies were always about families.

I did not have time to date in high school, but when I was a junior in nursing school, I met a medical student. Initially, he was nice and treated me as if I were special. We had our issues, but I thought we would get married.

All of a sudden, he did not return my phone calls. I was devastated and hurt. I did not hear from him for two months. One evening, I received a call from him and he apologized for his behavior and said he wanted to try again. I was happy and quickly accepted his apology.

Two months later on a nice Saturday evening, I was feeling happy to have a man who cared for me and spend time with. We were supposed to go out. He came to pick me up and said, "Tamuriat, I need to talk to you." He sat on the couch, and I wondered why he was sitting down when we were supposed to be going out.

He told me he had dated someone when we broke up, and she was now pregnant, and that his father had advised him to marry her. He gave me three choices. One, I could continue to see him, and he would get a divorce once the baby was born. Two, I could break up with him that night and never see him again. Before he could say the third choice, I stopped him. I told him to get out; we were done. I could not sleep that night. I felt like a fool. I was depressed for months.

Then I met another guy and we dated briefly. However, he felt that because I was a nurse and had a good salary and a nice condo, he shouldn't have to pay for anything when we went out. I dated another guy who was not dependable; he never showed up at the time he said he would, and sometimes he never showed up at all. Other guys were controlling and some were insecure. I also dated a guy who would downplay my accomplishments every chance he got; my self-esteem was almost down to nothing by the time I had the courage to break up with him.

I got my heart broken many times during my dating years. I met so many guys who were jerks, and at one point, I gave up dating altogether. I decided to focus on something constructive. I went back to graduate school; since I had already received my Masters of Science in Nursing, I decided to get my Masters of Business Administration. I also became an Authorized Outreach OSHA Safety Trainer and ServSafe Food Sanitation Safety Trainer. I have American Case Management Association Certification and National Surgical Quality Improvement Program Certification.

In the meantime, I learned that I had fibroids, a condition common among African American women. I had a fibroid embolization procedure, but it was a mistake. The fibroids came back, and the procedure further contributed to my inability of ever being able to conceive. Even when I get married, I could never conceive a child of my own. My doctor informed me that I had a 5 percent chance of ever having a child of my own. I had just had my thirty-ninth birthday with no prospect of getting married.

So I decided to look into an adoption. I signed up with an adoption agency and was assigned to a wonderful social worker named Susan. She came over to my house to conduct a home study. I remember her joking and saying, "You have such a lovely place here overlooking Chicago's Millennium Park; I wish you could adopt me." I passed the home inspections and the background checks. Then I found out that part of the process of adoption is to attend a class called Foster/Adoption Parent Training and get a certificate. I attended this class; I was very surprised to find out how many people wanted to have foster children only to receive a monthly check; there were few people who do it because they really care about having a child.

I completed the class and received my foster parent and adoption certificate necessary for adopting a child. After I received my certificate, I was introduced to three possible children for adoption, but none of these situations worked out. The social worker told me she would keep looking and would call me when a child was available. Usually there are fees involved, but these agencies had a program called the Black Children Adoption program, and I was only required to pay for legal fees to handle the process of the actual adoption.

While I was waiting for a child to become available for adoption, my fibroids were getting worse, and I was informed by my physician that I now needed myomectomy surgery to remove the fibroids. I had this surgery and was on medical leave for six weeks to recover. As I lay alone and in pain, I was crying and wondering if I would ever be able to conceive and whether I would ever meet someone who I would want to marry. One afternoon, as I lay there and my mind started wondering again, I received a phone call from Susan, the social worker.

"Tami, are you still interested in adopting a child?"

I responded emphatically, "Yes!"

She told me about a baby boy born that day and available for adoption. I thought I must be dreaming. After that call, I did not hear from her for two weeks. I went back to work, and on one Friday afternoon, I received a call from the social worker. She asked if I was still interested in adopting the boy she had told me about before and said I could go see him at his foster parent's house that evening. They were expecting the biological mother to sign the paperwork on Monday, and I could bring him home on that day. She told me I could go and buy a few baby items over the weekend, but to keep in mind that I might have to return them if the mother did not sign the papers on Monday

That Friday evening as I was driving to Naperville, I had a flat tire. I said to myself, "I have never had a flat tire before in my whole life, why today?" I also said to myself, "Nothing is going to jeopardize this adoption for me." I called the foster parent to let her know that there was a delay but I was still on my way. Then I called my insurance company who sent a man out to change the flat tire and replace it with the spare one in my trunk. It was now about 8:45 p.m. It was after 9:15 p.m. when I arrived at the foster parent's house.

I finally got to see this little boy. I fell in love with him the minute I saw him. That weekend, I bought a crib, diapers, a car seat, baby formula, and more, but left everything unopened just in case. Then I searched the Internet for a boy's name. I saw the name Ivan, meaning "a precious gift from God." I decided to name him Ivan.

On Monday afternoon when I was at work, I received the call from Susan.

"Congratulations! You are now a mother; the baby's biological mother just signed the paperwork."

I shared the news with my coworker Paula. She was so excited for me, she told me, "I will finish your work for you. Go ahead and go get your baby."

The late afternoon traffic to Naperville from downtown Chicago was horrible, but I did not care. When I got to the foster parents' home, the social worker was there to greet me. She and the foster parent helped me to put the baby in the car seat.

When I was driving Ivan back home, I kept looking back at him, saying to myself, "I cannot believe I have a baby in a backseat of my car. I am now a mother. What a wonderful dream come true!" I am still dreaming.

After I got accustomed to being a mother, I started dating again, even trying online dating. I was a single mother when I first met a man named Scott Gilbert. Scott was a kind, generous, family man. After we dated for a while, Scott told me he would adopt Ivan when we got married. I fell in love. A year later, we got married. Together, we now have three children. I have two wonderful stepchildren from Scott's previous marriage.

Exercise

In the following exercise, think about a time when you set a goal for yourself or you had a dream. And, while you were in the process of achieving that dream, you realized you would have to take different steps or a different direction to achieve it.

1. When did you feel like giving up on your dream of being in a happy relationship?

   _____

   _____

2. What can you do to continue to put yourself out there again and again until you find your prince and find that someone who will love you as much as you love him or her? List them, and do everything that you write down.

   _____

   _____

Lessons Learned

- I learned never to give up. I had many unsuccessful relationships, but I was determined to find my prince. As I was fighting against my age and my fibroid condition, I knew my chances of having children were decreasing. I always dreamt of being married and having a family of my own.

- I realized that a family does not have to look a certain way. I decided to adopt a child at the age of thirty-nine as a single woman. Eventually, I found a wonderful family man who loved me for who I am and with whom I fell deeply in love, and finally we became a family.

Figure 16. Tami and Scott's wedding day, July 18, 2010.

Chapter 8

The Joys and Challenges of Raising Children

Reflections

Being a mother is a joyous and rewarding experience. At the same time, being a mother has its challenges, from managing busy schedules, a job, and a household, to handling various issues that come with growing children and authorities in school systems. Children have minds of their own. In addition, other challenges in raising children include teaching morals and values; maintaining discipline so they will grow up to be good citizens and contributors to society; dealing with the financial aspects of raising children; and dealing with the educational system. Children come with many challenges; it is our job as parents to deal with these challenges effectively and in the best way possible. At the same time, you want to build and maintain bonds with your children in a loving manner. These bonds are what will help them trust and listen to you as you are trying to guide them. We, as parents, have to be our children's advocate at all times. Children need to know that we love them no matter what. What has helped me a lot in my parenting is that I constantly think about our children's future. Like Stephen Covey said, begin with the end in mine. I relate to my children now based on what relationship I would like to have with them in the future. My actions are consistent with my wanting to be respected and have great relationships with them when they become adults.

Being a mother is challenging, especially if you do not have close or extended family support nearby. My sister helped me with my son whenever she could. I had a few friends who also helped me out. After I had my son, I wished my mother was alive and here in the United States with me. I really envied my friends who had their mothers come and stay with them to help them out.

Another part of motherhood that I found difficult was making friends with other mothers to have play dates for my son. I felt like I was back in high school again. There is also a click among mothers. All the mother stay in their clicks; no one invites you in. As a new mother moving to a new area, it was hard.

As my son got older, being a mother of an African American boy became a challenge as well. I found myself having to constantly fight for him in the school system. After I got married and moved to the suburbs, my husband was happy to adopt my son. When Ivan started school, he was one of the few African American students in his class. He was a typical boy, energetic and active. I often volunteered in his first-grade class, and I would see most of the boys in the class being boys— that is, active. However, soon his teacher was calling me to relate different incidents in which Ivan misbehaved, such as pushing a student or taking a pencil from another child. When I would ask for the background or the context for the incident, the teacher never seemed to have answers for me.

Then the teacher sent me information about how she thought Ivan had ADD and he needed to be put on medication. I was already aware that African American boys are quick to be diagnosed with ADD, placed on medication, and then placed in special education classes. Being a nurse, I knew that these medications had side effects. I refused to have him labeled and given these medications; instead, I changed and monitored his diet, spent more time with him, and enrolled him in different sport activities. Looking back, I'm glad that I did not go along with labeling and placing him on ADD medication.

Then I was informed that the school needed to put him on a behavior plan and to do a daily observation; fill out a checklist on him on a daily basis. I asked the teachers if there were other boys in the school requiring the same daily observation. The answer was no.

The following is an e-mail sent to me from my son's school:

Dear Mr. and Mrs. Gilbert,

As a part of the process, a couple of staff members wrote up observations of Ivan. Our intervention specialist also jotted down some notes about what Ivan was doing while she was supporting some students in the classroom. Below is the sample observation:

Observation
4-6-2011

1:50 — When told to get water after gym, took his time, needed teacher's reminder
- Need teacher's reminder to attend On Rug time

1:55: — Playing with lint on the carpet
- Initiated on question
- Playing on the rug
- Last one to get up, once told to get back to seat

2:00: — Standing by the desk instead of sitting
- Talking to student sitting next to him
- Raised hand to ask teacher to help him spell a word
- Playing with pencils
- Tapping his feet, tapping on the table, and doing other little things

2:05: — Cued to get back to assignment
- Raised his hand and asked questions

2:10 — Staring at the pencil
- Writing on cup
- Asking questions

Other times:
- Dancing at his seat
- Writing words in his workbook
- Chatting with student across from him

– Cued to complete his assignment
– Didn't know where to put completed work

After a long conversation with a good friend who helped me through this difficult time, below is my response to their e-mail and Observation Report:

Dear Mrs. —

Thank you so much for the Observation Report on my son. I am certain that you are doing everything to see that he is being impartially observed, and that when compared with other children his age, his behavior is not atypical. The intense surveillance to which he is been subjected is possibly causing him to become increasingly self-conscious and tense. As a professional, I am sure you would agree that if your supervisor observed you minute-by-minute, and you knew that his/her comments would have a negative impact on you, you would become nervous and tense, also. The fact that he is a child and is functioning in an environment that is not altogether comfortable for him may also contribute to some of his behavior.

We work with him constantly at home. With all your help at school, his reading and math skills are improving; with much practice of spelling words Monday through Thursday every night, he does well on his spelling test every Friday. He reads his daily assigned books and word cards with very little assistance from us at home. Behaviorally and academically, looking at where he is now compared to his first day of first grade in August 24, 2010, he has made a major leap. This indicates to me that he does pay attention in class. Most of the behavior mentioned in your report seems to be the actions of a normal child who at times may be minimally distracted. I see no notations in your report that he is violent, hostile, or disobedient. He does not seem to be causing classroom disruption or giving the teacher a hard time. It appears that he is polite, does not yell or blurt out questions and comments, but raises his hand when he wants the teacher's attention, and he obeys commands from the teacher without resistance.

How does my son's behavior compare to that of other children his age? Is his behavior so different that it is causing problems for other students? It may be a little frustrating to the teacher. Is he always last in everything? How is playing with lint any different from other children pulling at their hair? Is his asking questions about the lesson or seeking assistance when he does not understand a concept wrong? Is he being held to a standard of perfection that is impossible for anyone to achieve—child or adult? I believe the bullet-point observations fall within the normal range of behavior of someone who is keenly aware that he is being watched and does not know why, but who senses that nothing good is going to come from these observations. No one should expect perfection of a child, just as no one expects perfection from an educator. Most of the behavior you mentioned in your observation can just as well be said about the majority of students in any classroom. If he perceives that he is being treated differently and is being punished for behavior that he sees other children exhibiting without being punished, this will cause him to become more tense. There are age-related parameters of activities that children fall into, and I think Ivan is within those parameters.

You continue to say that my son has behavior problems and he is not learning. Yet, the observed behavior mentioned in your report does not show that he is behaving so badly that he needs constant observation. Sending social workers to observe him to assist in making observable, necessary corrections is fine. But why are other teachers sent to observe him? Does it require an army of adults to observe one little boy? Also, following him around with a checklist of happy/sad faces everyday seems to be overkill, and it is definitely having a negative effect on him. He is aware that he is constantly being watched and is puzzled as to why he is being followed around and observed.

Please inform me specifically, what is your end-game for my son? What are you working toward doing with him? What I will not do is agree to have him shunted off into some special education program that I do not think he needs. He is smart, intelligent, and can perform as well as the average child his age. The stigma of having him diagnosed as behaviorally maladjusted will cause irreparable damage to him. I will not have him stigmatized this way. These observations are making him extremely tense, and he is beginning to dread going to school (he tells me every day he is sick and he wants to stay home from school). I would hope that as educators you would not want to contribute to his discomfort at school but instead would want to devise a plan of action that would help him. I am going to take this Observation Report to his pediatrician and get his opinion. I will also ask him to recommend additional professional help if he feels it is necessary.

I appreciate all of the positive assistance you gave me in assisting him to adjust to his classroom. I will cooperate in every way I can to see that he continues to perform well academically, and that his behavior continues to be age-appropriate. I don't think there are any perfect children, and he is no exception. I will continue to work with him so that he will develop into a well-adjusted, positive student. I hope that you have the same goal in mind for him.

After I sent this e-mail to the school and copied the principal, we had a meeting with the teachers, social worker, and the principal. After this meeting, the constant calling and complaints stopped. I also joined the school PTO board.

I chose to share with my son that he was adopted at a very young age when he could understand the concept. A friend recommended a book titled, I Wish for You. This book was excellent in helping explain to a child that he or she was adopted with love. This book helped me explain to him that adopting him was a dream come true, and that he is much wished for and wanted. I chose to tell him myself because I rather he heard it from me that he was adopted than from someone else.

When I got married, my husband had two children from his previous marriage, Evan and Erin. Being a stepmother was a challenge as well. Our whole family had a rough start. Then I realized that being children of a divorced parent is not easy, either. I thought about how going back and forth between two homes must be difficult for anybody, but especially children. When I was dating Scott and I would go to his house on the weekend, I remember how hard it was going back and forth, packing my necessities and clothes every weekend.

Going between two homes, in addition to having their dreams of living with their mother and father as a family ended by the divorce, must be very difficult. I really empathized with them. Once I had this realization, and my judgments of their behavior lessened, we began getting along better.

Speaking about my own mother, I missed not having my mother around when I was growing up in Nigeria and here in America. This is the reason that I have always encouraged my friends who are going through a rough period with their mothers to be patient and appreciate what they have with their mothers because I wish I had my mother around.

I was always lucky to have wonderful people who treated me like family. My husband's whole family immediately treated me as part of the family. My mother-in-law Barbara lives in California and sends me gift cards to special stores to treat myself; she has always encouraged me to take care of myself and take time to relax. My husband's Aunt Joyce and Uncle Richard accepted me as their niece and treated me like their own. I have never met anybody kinder and more generous than these two people. It feels nice and special to be spoiled once in a while. When I first moved to Highland Park, Aunt Joyce would come by and pick me up and show me around the city, the nice casual restaurants, where to do my grocery shopping, and where to shop for clothes and necessities. I love Aunt Joyce so much. Both Aunt Joyce and Uncle Richard love unconditionally. I am learning so much from them. I want to be just like them.

Exercise

As a parent, think about what challenges you are going through with your children and how you can effectively deal with them.

1. List the challenges you are facing with your children.

   _____

   _____

2. What actions can you take to effectively deal with those challenges?

_____

_____

3. Think of friends and professional agencies that can support you in dealing with the challenges that come in raising children.

_____

_____

Lessons Learned

- I learned to love children unconditionally. Dealing with most challenges that come with being a parent is easier when you come from a place of love.

- I learned to listen to my instincts about my children when dealing with authorities within the educational systems.

Figure 17. Erin, Ivan, and Evan.

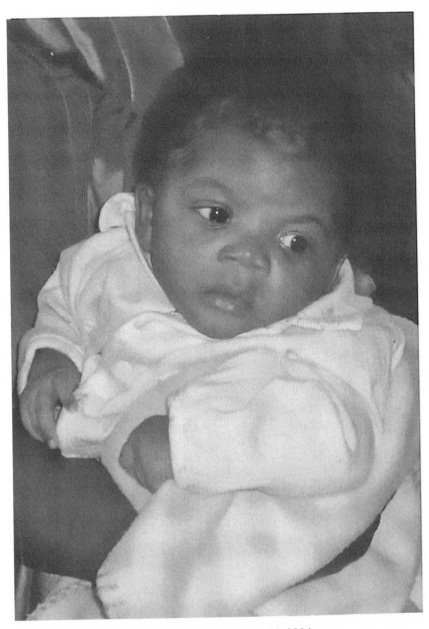

Figure 18. Ivan at 1 month old, 2004.

Chapter 9
Dreams Realized

Reflections

At some point in our lives, we review and evaluate where we have been and where we want to be in life. If we are not where we want to be, we must ask ourselves what we need to do to get there. At some point, we realize that we may have less years ahead of us than behind us. Before our dreams are realized, we run into many barriers and obstacles; the important thing is the lessons we learned along the way. You must be persistent and persevere to reach your dreams; you must not give up because you may be closer to your dreams than you realize.

I heard many times that if at first you don't succeed, try again, and again, and never ever give up. The following stories illustrate some of the incredible people who showed how even horrible tragedies and setbacks can help fuel a drive for success. These people never gave up on success. From Walt Disney's failed business ventures to Oprah Winfrey's abusive childhood, these people faced and overcame many obstacles. They have been through the meat grinder and came out even better than before.

Included here are the stories of businessmen and the companies they founded that are known around the world today, but their beginnings weren't always smooth.

Henry Ford, who is known today for his innovative assembly line and for American-made cars, was not an instant success. He failed many times with his early businesses and was broke five times before he founded the successful Ford Motor Company.

Figure 19. Henry Ford.

Today, Disney makes billions of dollars from merchandise, movies, and theme parks around the world, but Walt Disney himself had a rough start. He was fired by a newspaper editor because he was told that he lacked imagination and had no good ideas. Disney went on to start a number of businesses that didn't last too long and ended up in bankruptcy and failure. He didn't give up, he hung in there until he eventually found success that worked.

Figure 20. Walt Disney.

Many of the scientists and thinkers who are regarded as some of the greatest minds of our century often had to face great obstacles, the ridicule of their peers, and the animosity of society; for example, Albert Einstein was a genius who won a Nobel Prize and changed the face of modern physics. Einstein also had a rough start; he did not speak until he was four years of age and did not read until he was seven years old. His teachers, including his own parents, thought he was mentally handicapped. He was even expelled from one school and denied admission to an-other. But he, too did not give up on his purpose and dreams until he succeeded.

Figure 21. Albert Einstein.

Inventors have changed the face of the modern world, but not without a few failed prototypes along the way. The young Thomas Edison was told by his teachers that he was "too stupid to learn anything." He fared no better at work, as he was fired from his first two jobs for not being productive enough. Even as an inventor, Edison made 1,000, some said 10,000, unsuccessful attempts at inventing the lightbulb. The point I am trying to make is that Edison never gave up until he succeeded. When he was asked why he failed so many times, he responded, "I have not failed. I have just found 10,000 ways that won't work."

Figure 22. Thomas Edison.

Some public figures, from talk show hosts to politicians, have had a few failures before they came out on top; Oprah Winfrey, for example. Oprah is known to most people as one of the most iconic faces on TV as well as one of the richest and most successful women in the world. Oprah faced a difficult road getting to that position, however, enduring a rough and often abusive childhood. She also had numerous career setbacks, including being fired from her job as a television reporter because she was "unfit for TV." Now Oprah own her own TV station!

Figure 23. Oprah Winfrey.

Some actors, actresses, directors, and writers had their fair share of rejection and failure before they made it big on screen. All these stories show that all that work really does pay off with success in the long run. For example, Lucille Ball, during her career, had thirteen Emmy nominations, and she won it four times. Before starring in I Love Lucy, she was widely regarded as a failed actress and a B movie star. Even her drama instructors told her to try another profession because they felt she was not going to make it in Hollywood or anywhere else. As we know now, of course, she proved them all wrong.

Figure 24. Lucille Ball.

Even though Stephen King is now known as one of the best-selling authors of all time, his first book, the iconic thriller Carrie, was rejected thirty times, and he finally threw it in the trash. Luckily, his wife had enough faith in him to take the book out of the trash and encouraged him to re-submit it to another publisher–and the rest is history! King has written and pub-lished hundreds of best-selling books.

Figure 25. Stephen King.

While some athletes rocket to fame right away, others had to overcome many obstacles, like Michael Jordan. He is now known as the best basketball player of all time. But in high school, Jordan was cut from the basketball team! Jordan didn't let this setback stop him from playing the game and reaching his dream of becoming one of the best basketball players in the history of the NBA. Being cut from the team turned out to be his drive and motivation to practice and play harder.

Figure 26. Michael Jordan.

I am going to end this section with Jordan's famous quote:

"I have missed more than 9,000 shots in my career. I have lost almost 300 games. On 26 occasions I have been entrusted to take the game-winning shot, and I missed. I have failed over and over and over again in my life. And that is why I succeeded."

These stories stress one of the most important lessons of all: perseverance; *never ever give up on your dreams.*

As I write this chapter of this book, I still do OSHA and Food safety training and work for one of the best hospitals in the northern suburb of Chicago. I am starting my new adventures in an environment where everything and everyone is focused on improving people's lives. The staff's well-being is also a priority. I know there will be challenges, but my old job has prepared me to deal with whatever may come.

I continue to practice Ramadan every year. I both dread and look forward to Ramadan. It comes once a year and lasts thirty days. I dread Ramadan because I am not able to eat and socialize with friends and family during the day; we can only eat before sunrise and after sundown. I look forward to it because— beside the hunger I feel during the first two weeks—I always feel good due to the detox effect it has on me.

Ramadan occurs in the ninth month of the Islamic calendar. It is observed by Muslims worldwide as a month of fasting to commemorate the first revelation of the Quran to Muhammad according to Islamic belief. Ramadan's annual observance is regarded as one of the Five Pillars of Islam. The month lasts thirty days and is based on the visual sighting of the crescent moon. Sometimes, it only lasts twenty-nine days, but I have always prepared myself to do Ramadan for thirty days.

During the month of Ramadan, Muslims all over the world abstain from eating, drinking, and other physical activities during the daylight hours. Ramadan is much more than just not eating and drinking, though. This is also a time to purify the soul, refocus attention on God, and practice self-sacrifices. We as Muslims are called upon to use this month to reevaluate our lives in light of Islamic guidance and practices.

We are to make peace with those who have wronged us, strengthen ties with family and friends, and do away with our bad habits. In addition to the detoxification of our bodies, Ramadan helps us to cleanse our lives, our thoughts, and our feelings.

In addition to doing Ramadan every year, I also further discovered my spiritual side. I have faith and pray a lot. I practice Kundalini Yoga two to three times every week. I believe in angels and that when we call on them, they help us. My favorite angel is Archangel Michael; I believe he has helped me often.

A lot of good things have happened in my life. I did not like the house we lived in, but my husband and I were able to buy another house that we love. I was in a job I hated with no prospect of getting another. Now, I am in a much better situation. I have more free time and am making every effort to spend as much time as possible with my family. I do not have to get up as early as I did to go to work, and I have more time and energy to spend with my family and friends. I have everything that I have always wanted. I feel truly blessed.

I am married to a wonderful man and have three wonderful children. I cannot imagine my life without my family. My husband Scott is kind and patient; he is truly a man who values his family and would do anything for us. He is also a wonderful husband who loves me unconditionally and always supports me, no matter what. As family, we enjoyed going on vacation together to different places like Mexico, Arizona, Newport Beach, Palm Desert, and so on.

My son Ivan is such a smart boy, too wise for his age. He keeps my husband and me very busy, always trying to outsmart us. He is now in junior high, doing well, and comes home every day saying how much he loves school. I always said to myself, "Thank God," and I hope he continues to love school.

My stepson Evan and I had a rough start when my husband and I first met, but we have come a long way since his father and I got married. Evan is very funny, fun to be around, and very smart. I admire his academic achievements and how responsible he is. He keeps up with his school work and still has a busy social life on the weekends.

My stepdaughter Erin is smart and very family oriented. She is also a great student and keeps up with her homework and grades without any nagging from her parents. Erin has a kind heart and is very thoughtful. Every time she goes away, she is always thinks of everyone and brings us back thoughtful presents.

I love my spiritual friends Maria and Rasa. My neighbor Maria once said to me, "You have passed the test." She listened to the story I told her about my life and what I went through and told me she thought it was a test from God. I "passed" and have learned a great deal, which will help me in the future.

In the meantime, today I enjoy what I have—a fulfilling career and most importantly, a loving, wonderful family who I enjoy spending time with. I feel truly blessed.

Exercise

In this exercise, think about all your accomplishments, how you accomplished them, acknowledge them, and celebrate them.

1. Think about all your accomplishments and write them down.

   _____

   _____

2. How did you celebrate these accomplishments? If you haven't already, how do you plan to celebrate your accomplishments?

   _____

   _____

3. Think about how you can help other people accomplish their goals and dreams.

   _____

   _____

Lessons Learned

- I learned to be humble about my accomplishments.

- I learned to acknowledge, reflect on, and celebrate my accomplishments.

- I learned to look for ways to give back and help other people to achieve their goals and dreams.

- I learned to slow down and enjoy life more; life is too short not to be enjoyed.

- I learned to work to live, not to live to work. I worked so hard all my life, now it is time to relax a little.

Figure 27. Tami's family; Ivan, Erin, Evan, and Scott

Chapter 10

Helping People Achieve Their Goals

Reflections

A number of strategies have helped me achieve my goals and dreams, and I am confident that these tactics will help you as well if you practice them. The number one strategy that contributed to my success is perseverance. I feel fortunate to have people who helped me along the way as well. The first step in goal setting and achieving your dreams is that you really have to want to achieve these goals. I think the starting point of all achievement is desire.

My Formula for Success:

Desire + Vision + Action + Perseverance = Success

has worked for me as well as for many other people.

Once you establish your goals, then you must commit to them by identifying the critical paths to take to reach them. You must create action plans and steps to take with time lines. Then on a regular basis, you must evaluate and check to see if you are on track to reaching your goals. If you are on track— great! If you are not, you must look at why you are not, learn from it, course correct, and continue to move on.

Visualization is also critical to your success in achieving your goals. Visualize yourself achieving your goals and how that would make you feel; how much better your life will be after you have become successful in achieving your goals.

93

It's been quite a journey. I have learned a lot in my life to achieve all my dreams, and now I am here to help other women do the same, to overcome their obstacles to achieving their dreams and reaching their goals. We all get discouraged; it is important to get back on track.

I have helped coach other people. Here are some examples of people I have helped.

I supported Donna when she was struggling with graduate school. Donna decided to go back to school to get a master of science in nursing degree. From what she said, the program was very challenging, and at times she felt just like giving up. Donna and I spoke on the phone or met for lunch once a month; with my encouragement and help keeping her on track, she received her degree.

Renee got laid off the job she had worked at for eight years. After Renee got over the shock of losing her job, she reached out to me. I was able to talk to her once a week, helped her get clear on what she would like to do next, what she has passion for, and that was to be a nurse. Then I spent a whole day with her, helping her write down her plans to reach this newly set goal of becoming a registered nurse.

Renee wrote down step-by-step action plans. For example, she had to research different nursing schools, decide whether she preferred classroom or online classes, and choose a school. She had to determine what financial aid was available, whether she would be able to work another job part-time and go to school full-time, or go to school part-time and work full-time. Renee set time lines for every action plan. Now, we talk once a week to touch base, talk about her progress, where she is taking action, and where she has stopped taking action toward her goal of becoming a registered nurse. Renee is now in her second year of a nursing program, doing well, and on track.

Another young woman felt stuck in a job she hated and was looking into becoming a food safety training instructor/proctor. I coached her through the steps she needed to take to become a food safety trainer. She took the exam to get her state license, she passed, and now she is officially a ServSafe Food Safety trainer.

Sharon was tired of dating a lot of jerks. She went out a lot, hoping to meet a nice guy, but it was just not happening. I encouraged her not to give up if her dream was to have a loving relationship or to find her soul mate. I asked her if she had ever thought about online dating, and she said she was open to trying it. I gave her an assignment to research several reputable online dating sites. After she posted her photo and completed her profile, she started getting responses from the dating site. We have a call once every two weeks to talk about any area in which she may be stalled. She has been dating a nice guy for about seventeen months now and he treats her like queen; he was the one. Sharon is now engaged to be married.

Linda was married twice and both marriages were terrible. As we talk, she admits she isn't ready to give up on love. We work on what actions she can take to find the love that she deserves. She writes down two actions to take weekly toward finding her soul mate. I was surprised when during our monthly call, she said that she had met a man who she plans to marry. After a few months had passed, she called to tell me she and this guy had gotten married. I was shocked but happy for her. Now, it has been four and a half years, and they are still in love and happily married.

Exercise

Think about your life—what goals and dreams you have that you are committed to being realized.

1. Right now, are you where you want to be in your life?

   Yes or No

2. What goals and dreams would you like to be successful in achieving? List them below.

   _____

   _____

3. What actions can you take today toward becoming successful in achieving these goals?

_____

_____

4. What support do you think you will need to achieve your goals? List them below (such as a friend who will hold you accountable, a consultant, a coach, etc).

_____

_____

Lessons Learned

- I learned that with a desire in my heart and the courage to persevere, I can accomplish any goals that I set for myself and become successful.

- I also learned that when I am blessed with a skill and have discovered the strategies to accomplish my goal successfully, I am obligated to help others do the same.

- I learned that to give back and help others is rewarding.

Appendix 1
Essential Lessons Learned

- Perseverance helped me get where I am now. It helped me create a life I wanted. I learned not to give up.

- No matter what happened, I learned to move forward in life and accomplish what I set my mind to do, which was to accomplish my goals and dreams.

- I refused to stay in a condition of poverty and low self-esteem. I learned to move on and prosper in the face of adversity and racism. I refused to be belittled and made to feel like nothing.

- I learned the importance of taking time to develop solid friendships.

- I discovered ways to create the life I wanted. I mastered essential techniques to get a career I wanted, a baby, a husband, and a family.

- I learned how important it is to have the highest education you can possibly have. For me, education was a ladder out of the basement and poverty.

- Most of all, I learned to have faith and get close to God. Prayer has helped me a lot. I strongly recommend watching and listening to Joel Osteen, who taught me to have faith in God, and that God already has different people in place to help us accomplish our dreams and hopes.

Appendix 2
Tips for a Happier Life

- Be accountable. If you have failed at something, admit it to yourself. But don't beat yourself up over it.

- Don't wallow too long in self-pity. We all fail at something.

- It's not about how you fell; it is how you pick yourself back up.

- Always look at obstacles and barriers as opportunities.

- If you made mistakes that led to failure, consider what you would do differently if you had the chance to do it over again; then do it over again when you get that chance.

- Always consider failure as a learning experience.

- You can never succeed if you don't fail at times. Failure has made many great people become even more dedicated to achieving their goals. Consider Thomas Edison who encountered failure many times before he finally invented electricity. Consider Oprah Winfrey, Walter Disney, Henry Ford, Albert Einstein, and many others who moved passed their obstacles against all odds.

- Forgive others who may have hurt you or caused you to fail.

- Most importantly of all, forgive yourself.

- Have faith.

- Be determined.

- Eliminate self-doubt.

- Find a mentor who has walked down the same road that you want to walk down.

- Avoid situations and people who might lead you to the bottom of the well again.

- Remember where you have been and where you are going.

- Keep a mental picture of your goals and of what life will be like for you someday when you reach them.

- Never lose hope.

- If you backslide, try again. Never stop trying.

- Lean on your strong and supportive friends, but don't be too needy. No one likes to be around needy people.

- Maintain positive thoughts.

- Remind yourself that you are not a victim.

- Most importantly, remove toxic and unhealthy people from your life.

- Keep aggressive family members at a distance.

- Start each day with a prayer or word of thankfulness.

- Play soft, relaxing, and beautiful background music.

- Learn to be accepting of those who are different.

- Feed your body with the healthiest food you can afford.

- Talk about yourself in positive ways.

- Acknowledge compliments; don't dismiss them; just say, "Thank you."

- Dust yourself off when you fall; get back up with confidence, not self-pity.

- Find time for yourself; spend time to take care of yourself. Celebrate the victories of others (and yes, other women).

- Mentor the young and those less fortunate.

- Volunteer your time.

- Stay in contact with your Higher Power.

- When you achieve a goal, celebrate in your own way.

- Take a risk and do something you have always dreamed of doing.

- Be persistent in life; with perseverance, you will overcome and resolve the obstacles that stand in the way of your satisfying life.

Acknowledgments

Coming to Chicago at the age of fifteen and not being able to speak English, not knowing anyone in this strange city except my father, I would not have survived or be where I am today without the help of many people, including my sister, brother, teachers, neighbors, and friends.

I wish to begin by thanking my father for bringing me to America where I had the opportunity to receive an education; my late Aunt Fatilat, who taught me the value of education; my sister, Risikat Munson, for always being there for me and for her friendship; my brother, Olu Olabode, who helped me out whenever he could; and my half-sisters, Faosat and Basirat Olabode, for their support.

I owe deep gratitude to Scott Gilbert, my husband, for believing in me and for always supporting me even when he did not agree with me. He took a stand for me. I would not be where I am today without him. I also want to thank our children Ivan, Evan, and Erin for their love and support. Mrs. Joyce and Mr. Richard Hirsch, thank you for your unconditional love. Mrs. Barbara Gilbert, David Hirsch, Gary Gilbert, Samuel Gilbert, and Andy Hirsch, thank you for welcoming me into your family. Janella Merkson, Paula and Dave Farrell, thank you for being a kind and thoughtful friends and for all your support. Chandra Castaldo, thank you for always remembering my son's birthday every year, this meant a lot.

I want to acknowledge and thank the following people: my teacher from Harlan High School, Mrs. Mary Dixon, who is now my friend and supporter; she took an interest in me, showed me kindness, and provided me light in my darkest days; the late Mrs. Inez Smith, who opened her home, took me and my sister into her home, and welcomed us into her family when we really needed one; Rona House for always being there when I needed her and for being a good friend; Mary, Evelyn, and Karen, who worked with me as a team when I was working as a certified nursing assistant in Manorcare Nursing Home; and Lucy and Roy Murray, who also welcomed me into their home and family when I was almost homeless.

Special thanks to Lavanya Delayney, my first real, genuine friend I had in Chicago when I did not know anyone else or the American culture at the time. Lavanya accepted me unconditionally without any judgments. She treated me like her sister. I am very grateful to her.

I would not have accomplished the many milestones and different occasions in my life without Alexis Christie, Larinda Dixon, Lynn Williams, Seeta Durjan Begui, Marilyn Richard, and Jacqui Grullion; many thanks for their friendship and support.

Thanks to Barry Carr, Emelda Jones, Jerry Cox, Annette Singletary, Audrey Benford, Lorna Delgado, Candice Benton, Chandra Castaldo, Brenda Henson, Sherita Davis, and Ethel Walton for being there for me during my darkest hours when I was working in corporate America. To Ja'Vonne Harley, thank you for your ideas and inspiring conversations; you taught me so much and always had the courage to disagree with me when you thought I was wrong. To Dian Solari, for teaching me the value of having different resources; for teaching me to believe in the dream of living a better life. I learned from Dian to always be good to myself, to treat myself as I would expect to be treated by others. Larinda Dixon, you taught me how to be a true friend even when we had disagreements. Charlene Roderick, for teaching me to be kind to other people weather you know them or not; the value of giving back to society; the value of volunteering my time to help other people. Tayo and Joe Sosan, your friendship and help meant so much to me when I first moved to Highland Park, IL. Nagawa Kakumba and Nola Akala, thank you for your parental advice. Janella Merkson, Paula and Dave Farrell, thank you for being kind and thoughtful friends and for all your support. Chandra Castaldo, thank you for always remembering my son's birthday every year; this means a lot to him.

Kijsa Phillips, my new friend in Highland Park, thank you for your support, for showing me what a genuine and honest friendship is. Richard Phillips, you and Kijsa have a beautiful family. Thank you for welcoming my family into yours and supporting our family.

My gratitude to Trinity Christian College in Palos Heights for giving me a second chance at reaching my dream of getting my bachelor of science in nursing degree, which led to getting my advance degrees as well.

I want to acknowledge the Landmark Education program and everyone that participated with me in the program. This program helped me to put the past in the past, forgive those that I needed to forgive, release my childhood anger, and to move forward in my life. I owe most of my accomplishments to the Landmark Education program and their participants.

Leslie Fonteyne, my spiritual advisor, thank you for always reminding me what an extraordinary person I am and getting me back on track to the commitments in my life. You have worked wonders for me and my family.

Special thanks to Linda Ellis Eastman and Steve Harrison's team at Quantum Leap—Geoffrey Berwing, Martha Bullen, Brian Edmonson, Raia King, and Tamra Nashman—for your dedication, insight, guidance, and support, which helped me complete this book.

I have been very fortunate over the years to have had so many friends who have supported me through thick and thin. I cannot name you all; I apologize if I forgot to mention your name, but you know who you are. Thank you for always being there for me and for surrounding me with your warmth, love, and understanding.

About the Author

Tami Olabode Gilbert, RN, MSN, MBA, Author, Outreach OSHA Trainer, ServSave Food Sanitation Safety Trainer

Tami Gilbert is a native of Nigeria with a background in health care. Tami was brought to America by her father in search of a better education and a better life. Tami always dreamed of achieving the American success story of professional and personal accomplishments. Tami went on to earn her MSN and MBA degrees because she realized that education was the way out of her struggles. Through struggle and persistence, she has achieved her dream of becoming a professional, a wife, and a mother. In addition to being an author, she works in the Hospital in Quality Improvement Department contributing to the best practices of delivering better and safer surgical care to patients nationally. She is also a safety expert who specializes in decreasing workplace injuries, an OSHA trainer and a motivational speaker. Tami is an International Advisory Board member of the Professional Woman Network and Professional Woman Speakers Bureau.

Tami Gilbert is available to conduct seminars, workshops, and keynote speeches for corporations, nonprofit organizations, women's groups, and community groups. The topics she speaks on include the following:

- Goal-Setting Strategies that Ensure Your Success

- Don't Take NO for an Answer—My True Story of Overcoming Impossible Odds

- Make Your Dream Job a Reality—The 7 Steps to Finding the Employment You Desire

- Discover Your Soul Mate—Real Strategies to Find Your Life Companion

- How to Survive Both Child and Adult Bullying

- Improving Your Poor Employment Situation: What to Do.

- Overcoming the Past to have a Solid and Productive Future.

Coaching Services Available

Living a successful life doesn't come by accident. It only comes to those who invest time in learning exactly how to make it happen. The *Achieve Your Dream* coaching program includes webinars, one-to-one coaching, and group coaching to provide opportunities for people to learn from each other.

This coaching program will help you learn how to choose your goals, put action plans into place, track your progress toward your goals, and achieve your dreams.

For additional information, contact Tami at info@tamigilbert.com

Figure 30. Tami and Scott on vacation, 2010.

56562995R00073

Made in the USA
Charleston, SC
25 May 2016